Seasonal Knits

Guide to Knit All Year Long for Beginners

Copyright © 2020

All rights reserved.

DEDICATION

The author and publisher have provided this e-book to you for your personal use only. You may not make this e-book publicly available in any way. Copyright infringement is against the law. If you believe the copy of this e-book you are reading infringes on the author's copyright, please notify the publisher at: https://us.macmillan.com/piracy

Contents

Spring 1

    Brioche Stitch 1

    Socks 7

    Contton Candy Hat 24

Summer 31

    Drawstring Bag 32

    Pillow 37

    Tank 41

Fall 31

    Dishcloth 35

    Pumpkin 54

    Baby Sweater 62

Winter 81

    Beanie 70

    Scarf 78

    Leg Warmers 81

Spring

Brioche Stitch

SET UP ROW

Hold the yarn in front of your work, insert your right needle purlwise into the first stitch on your left needle and slip it off.

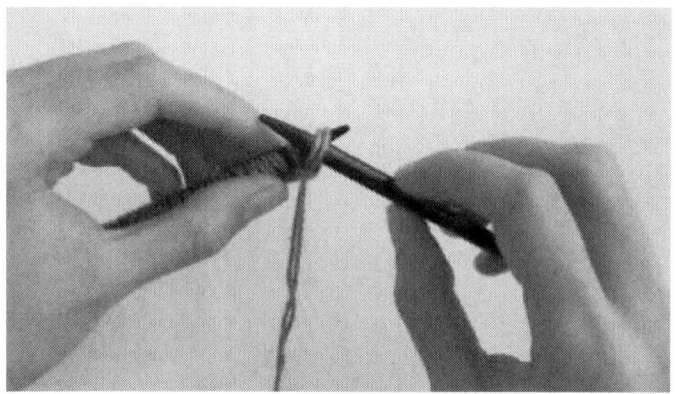

Bring the yarn over your right needle to the back of your work (this is called a 'yarn over').

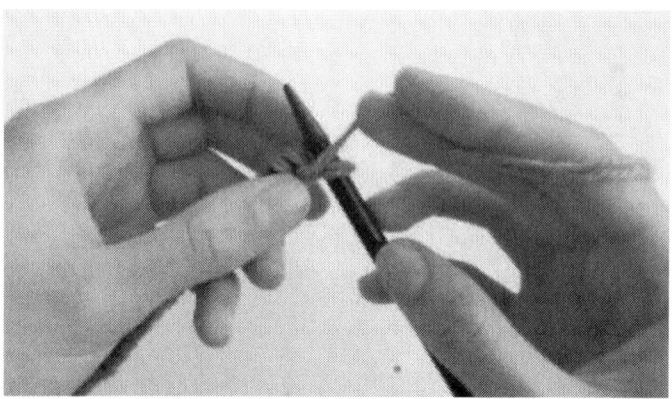

Knit 1 stitch as normal.

Repeat these 3 steps until you have worked all the stitches of your row.

PATTERN ROW

Hold the yarn in front of your work and slip 1 stitch purl-wise.

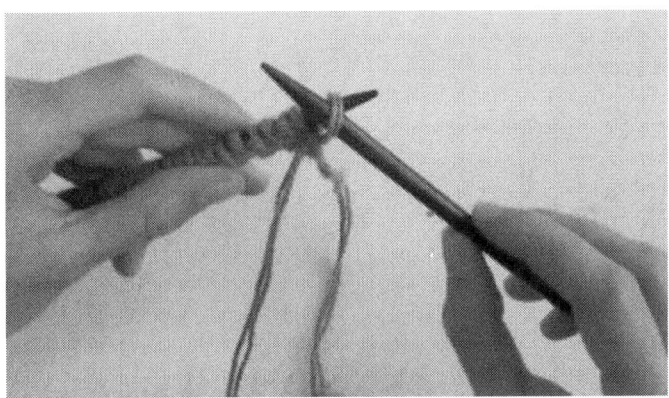

Make a yarn over.

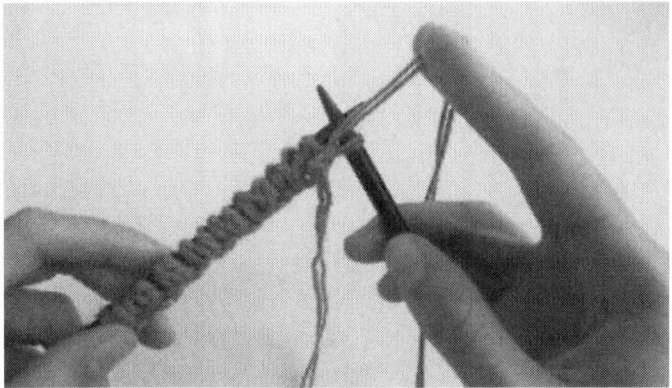

Knit the next stitch and the yarn over which sits in front of it together.

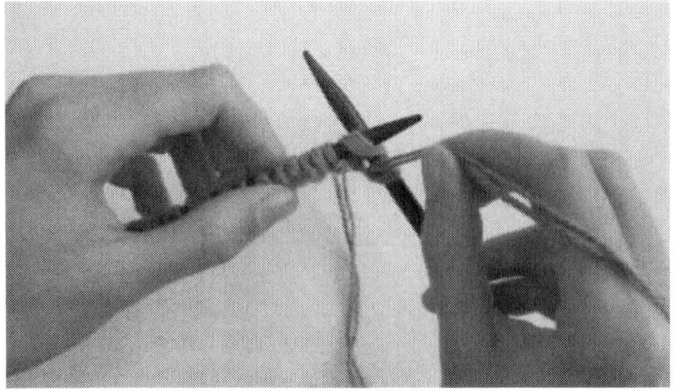

Repeat these 3 steps until you have worked all the stitches of your row.

Keep repeating this pattern row to keep working in brioche stitch, it couldn't be simpler!

CASTING OFF IN BRIOCHE STITCH

Casting off in brioche stitch is slightly different from normal, when you have finished knitting, follow the steps below to see how to cast off your stitches.

Purl 1 stitch.

Insert your right needle through the next stitch and the yarn over which sits in front of it and knit the 2 together.

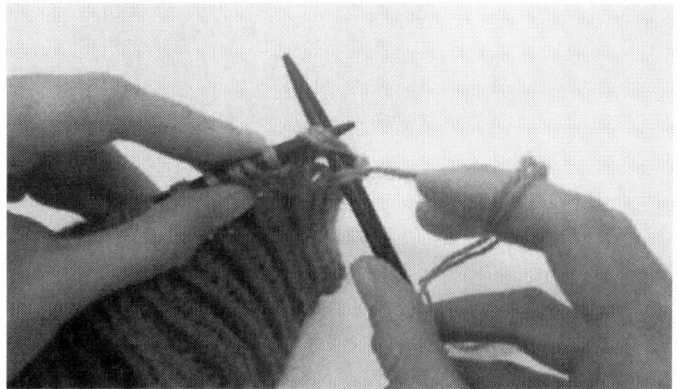

Use the tip of the left needle to lift the first stitch over the last one and off the right needle.

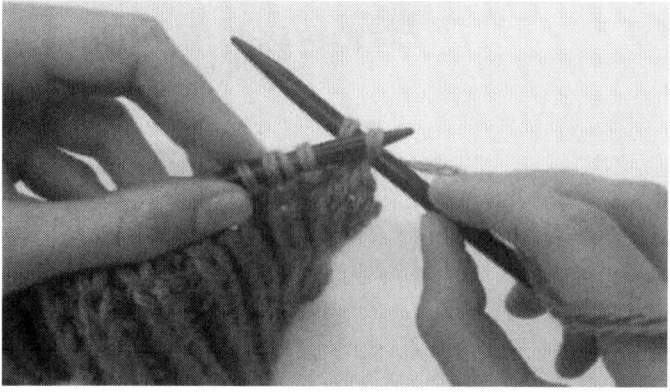

Keep repeating these steps until all of your stitches are cast off.

Socks

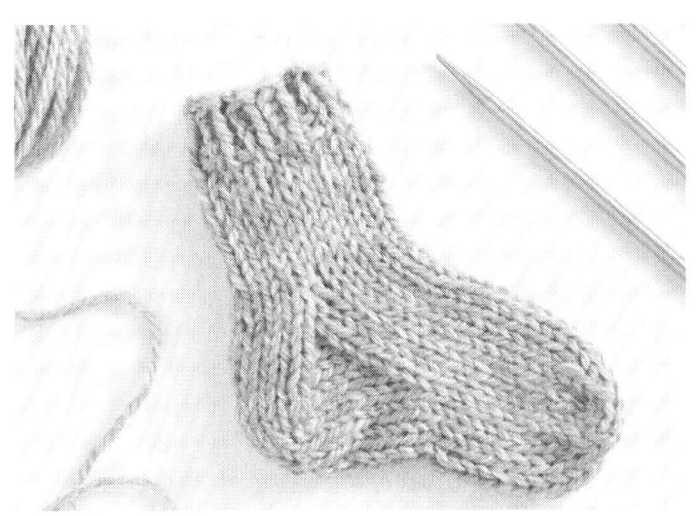

What You'll Need

Equipment / Tools

- 1 Pair of scissors
- 1 Yarn needle
- 1 Ruler or tape measure
- 1 Size-7 US double-pointed needles (set of 4)

Materials

- 1 Scrap of worsted weight yarn, about 20 yards

Steps to Make It

1.   Cast on and Join in Round

To begin, cast on 20 stitches onto one needle.

- Distribute the stitches onto three of the four needles.
- Slide the stitches to the end of the needle, beginning with the first cast on stitch.
- Slip 7 stitches one at a time onto another needle.
- Slip the next 6 stitches onto a third needle.

Once the stitches are evenly distributed, join the work in the round.

- Slip the first cast on stitch onto the needle with the last cast on stitch.
- Slip the last stitch over the first stitch and onto the last needle.

At this point, you can slip a stitch holder onto the needle to mark the end of the row. Or, you can note where the tail from your cast on is; this is the end of the row.

Seasonal Knits

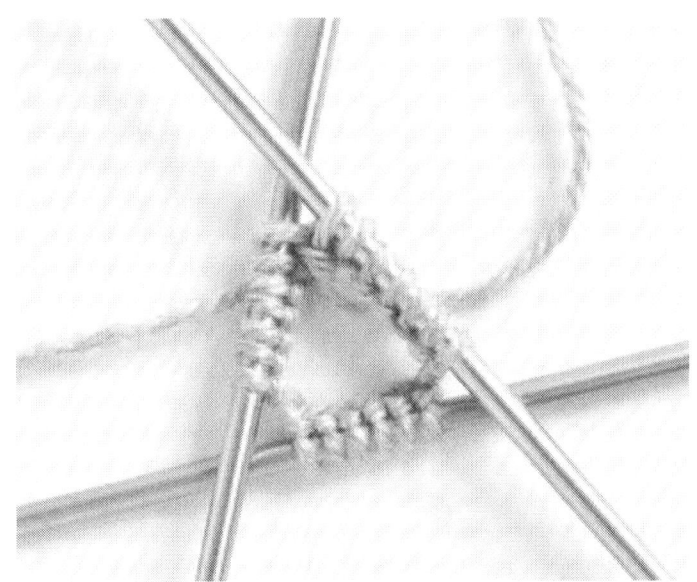

2. Knit the Ribbing

Work in knit 1, purl 1 ribbing for 4 rounds.

Use the fourth needle to work across the stitches on one needle. After that needle is empty, use it to work across the next needle, and so on.

If you're new to double-pointed needles, you might need to knit a little slower than usual. Once you've knit a couple of rounds, the work will begin to flow and feel much more stable.

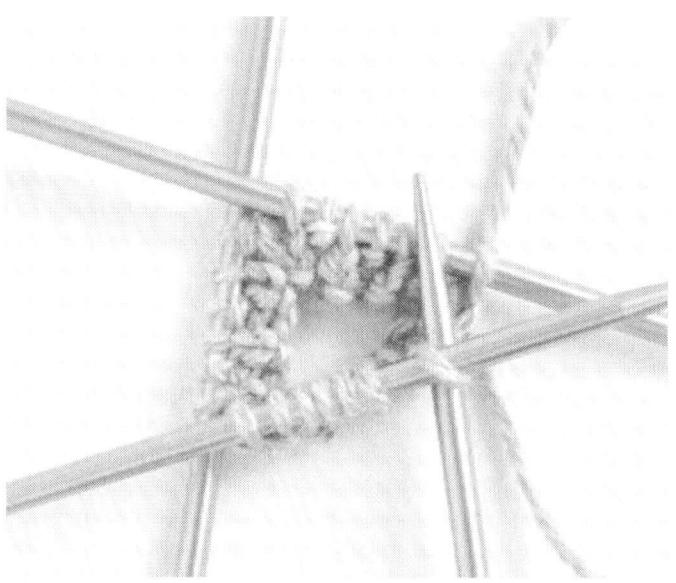

3. Knit the Leg

Knit every round for one inch. When knitting in the round, knitting every row produces stockinette stitch.

The leg is the part of the sock that often has interesting stitch patterns or cables worked into it. But when you're first learning, simple stockinette makes it easier to get started.

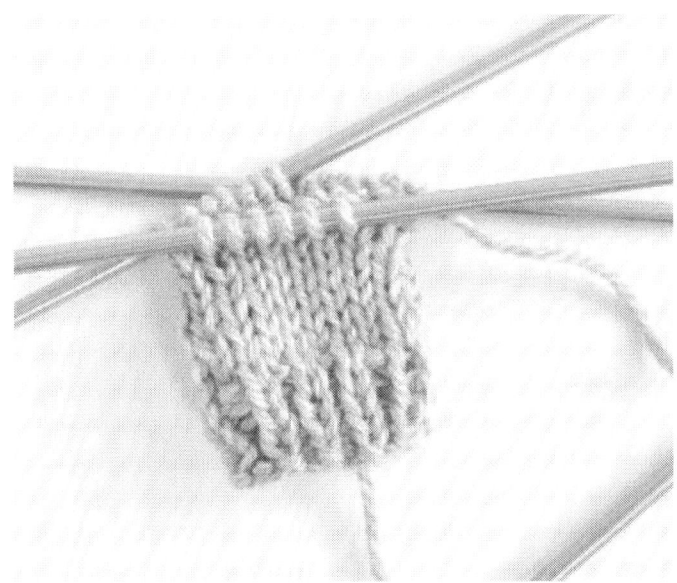

4. Knit the Heel Flap

There are different methods for knitting a heel, but one of the most common is using a heel flap and then "turning the heel."

- Knit the first 10 stitches of the round onto one needle.

- To make it easier to work with, slip the other 10 stitches onto one needle and allow them to hang while you work on the other stitches.

Knit the heel flap with a two-row repeat:

- Row 1 (wrong side): Slip the first stitch purlwise with the yarn in front, purl the rest of the stitches.
- Row 2: Slip the first stitch purlwise with the yarn in back, knit the rest of the stitches.
- Repeat these two rows 4 more times, until you've worked 10 rows total, ending on the knit side.

Seasonal Knits

5. Turn the Heel

Turning the heel is a common method for making the cup your heel sit in when you wear the sock. This method uses short rows, turning the work and knitting back over the stitches you just worked without knitting across the whole row.

As before, slip the stitches purlwise with the yarn in front.

- Row 1: Slip 1, purl 5, purl 2 together, purl one. Turn the work, leaving one stitch unworked.
- Row 2: Slip 1, knit 3, slip, slip, knit (SSK), knit 1. Turn the work, leaving one stitch unworked.
- Row 3: Slip 1, purl 4, purl 2 together. Turn the work. There are no unworked stitches.
- Row 4: Slip 1, knit 4, SSK. There are no unworked stitches. Six stitches remain on the needle.

Seasonal Knits

6. Pick Up Stitches and Divide Them Again

The gusset of a sock knits the leg stitches and the heel stitches back together. It shapes the sock so it fits around the heel and the top of the foot.

- Take an empty needle and pick up and knit six stitches along the side of the heel flap. The stitches should be easy to find because they are the slipped stitches along the edge of the heel flap.
- Use another needle to knit across the 10 stitches of the leg you left unworked as you made the heel flap.
- Use the newly empty needle to pick up and knit six stitches along the second side of the heel flap. Knit three of the stitches from the heel itself.
- Slip the last three stitches of the heel onto the needle with the first stitches you picked up. Use the newly empty needle and knit the three slipped stitches, along with the first stitches you picked up.

Seasonal Knits

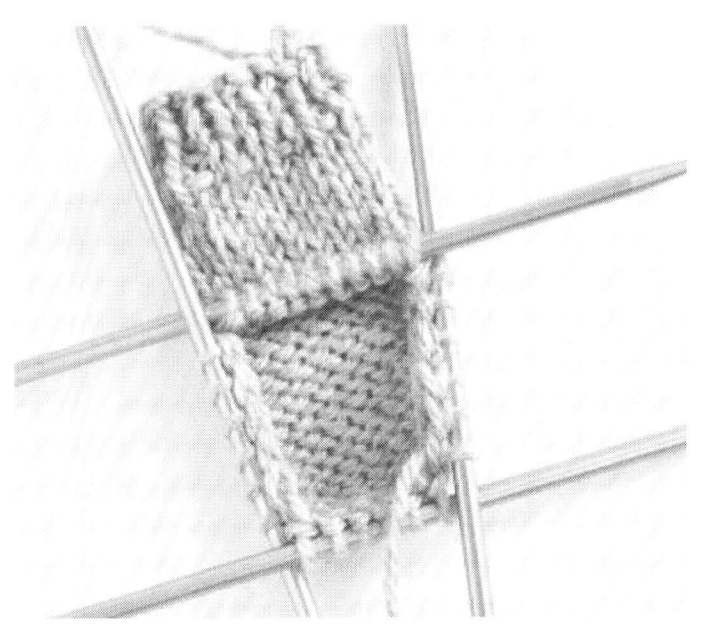

7. **Work the Gusset**

The stitches from the leg are on needle one, the next needle is needle 2, and the needle you just finished knitting is needle 3.

Now it's time to shape the gusset.

- Row one: Knit across the first needle. On the second needle, knit 1, SSK, and knit to the end of the needle. On the third needle, knit to within 3 stitches of the end of the row, knit two together, and knit the last stitch.
- Row 2: Knit every stitch.
- Repeat these two rows until you have five stitches on each of the second and third needles; 20 stitches total.

Seasonal Knits

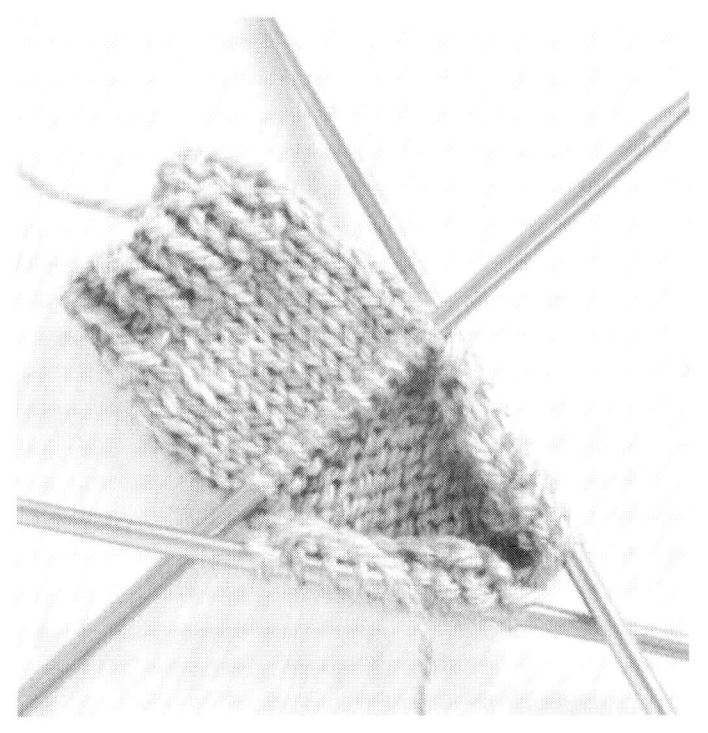

8. Knit the Foot

Once you have the gusset shaped and are back to 20 stitches, knit every stitch in every round for another inch. This makes the foot part of the sock.

9. Knit the Sock Toe

Now shape the toe of the sock. As before, the stitches on the top of the sock are on needle one, followed by needle two and needle three.

- Row 1: On needle one, knit 1, SSK to the last three stitches, knit 2 together, knit 1. On needle two, knit 1, SSK, and knit to the end. On needle three, knit to the last three stitches, knit 2 together, knit 1.

- Row 2: Knit every stitch.
- Row 3: Repeat row 1. You will have 12 stitches remaining.
- Slip the stitches from needle two onto needle three so that you have two needles with 6 stitches each.

10. Finish the Sock

To finish the sock, practice the standard way of closing off a sock, known as grafting or the Kitchener stitch. Weave in the ends.

Button Candy Hat

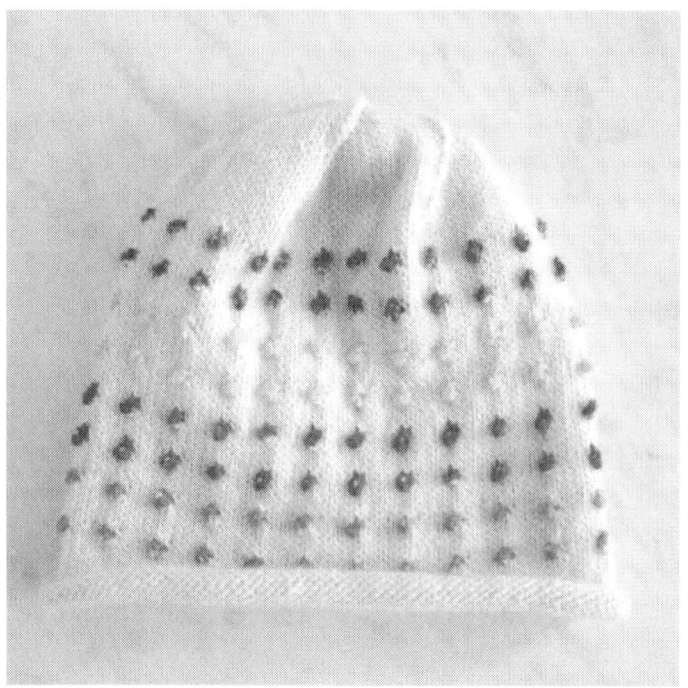

MATERIALS

- Main Color (MC): 1 skein of Purl Soho's Line Weight, 100% merino wool, in the color Heirloom White.
- Contrast Colors: 4 skeins of Koigu Premium Merino Needlepoint Yarns, 100% merino wool, in the colors (shown above, from left to right)…

Contrast Color a (CCa): 1145, Contrast Color b (CCb): 2229, Contrast Color c (CCc): 2100, Contrast Color d (CCd): 1504

- US #4, 12-inch circular needles or double pointed needles
- US #2, 12-inch circular needles
- A set of US #2 double pointed needles

GAUGE

8 1/4 stitches and 11 rows = 1 inch in stockinette stitch, using the MC and the smaller needles

SIZES

Newborn (Baby, Toddler)

- Circumference: 12 (14, 15 3/4) inches
- Height: 6 1/4 (7, 7 3/4) inches

NOTES

MB [make bobble]: knit into front and back (kfb), turn work, (with wrong side facing) k2tog, turn work, (with right side facing) k1 through the back loop (k1 tbl)

If you wish to modify the pattern, be sure to cast on a multiple of 5 stitches.

BEGIN

With larger needles and MC, cast on 100 (115, 130) stitches.

Place marker and join for working in the round being careful not to twist the stitches.

Knit one round.

Change to smaller needles.

Continue working in stockinette stitch, knitting each round, until the piece measures 1/4 (3/4, 1 1/4) inches from rolled edge.

MAKE BUTTON CANDY

Round 1: *With MC, k4; with CCa, make bobble (MB, see pattern notes above), repeat from * to end of round. Cut CCa.

Round 2: *With MC, k4, k1 through the back loop (k1 tbl), repeat from * to end of round.

Rounds 3-6: With MC, knit.

Repeat Rounds 1-6 one more time.

Repeat Rounds 1-6 two more times, with CCb in place of CCa.

Repeat Rounds 1-6 two more times, with CCc in place of CCa.

Repeat Rounds 1-6 two more times, with CCd in place of CCa.

SHAPE TOP OF HAT

Round 1 (Decrease Round): *K18 (21, 24), k2tog, place maker (pm), repeat from * to end of round. [95 (110, 125) stitches]

Round 2: Knit.

Round 3 (Decrease Round): *Knit to two stitches before marker, k2tog, repeat from * to end of round. (5 stitches decreased)

Repeat Rounds 2 and 3 one more time. [85 (100, 115) stitches]

Repeat Round 3 fourteen (seventeen, twenty) more times. [15 (15, 15) stitches]

FINISH

Cut yarn and thread it onto a tapestry needle to draw through remaining stitches. Pull tight and bring tail to inside of hat to weave in.

Weave in the remaining ends and gently block.

Summer

Drawstring Bag

Step: 1

GETTING STARTED:

Download the PDF for a set of portable project instructions. Read through all of the instructions before beginning.

ABBREVIATIONS:

BO—bind off; cm—centimeter(s); CO—cast on; k—knit; k2tog—knit 2 sts together; mm—millimeter(s); oz—ounce(s); pm—place marker; p—purl; RS—right side; rnd(s)—round(s); sl—slip; st(s)—stitch(es); wyif—with yarn in front; WS—wrong side; yd—yard(s); yo—yarn over

SIZE:

17" (43 cm) circumference x 9 1/2" (24 cm) high

MATERIALS:

- #4 medium weight yarn: Red Heart Super Saver (100% acrylic, 5 oz/141 g, 244 yd/223 m): #3955 Wildflower (A) 1 skein, Contrast color yarn (B) about 10 yds (9 m)
- Boye® size US 7 (4.5 mm) 16" (40 cm) circular needle
- Boye® size US 7 (4.5mm) double-pointed needles
- Stitch marker

- Yarn needle

See the Supply List for items you can purchase here.

GAUGE:

18 sts and 31 rnds = 4" (10 cm) in Half Linen Stitch. Gauge is not critical for this project.

PATTERN STITCHES:

HALF LINEN STITCH (MULTIPLE OF 2)

Rnds 1 and 3: Knit.

Rnd 2: *K1, sl 1 purlwise wyif; rep from * around.

Rnd 4: *Sl 1 purlwise wyif, k1; rep from * around.

Rep Rnds 1-4 for pattern.

Step: 2

DIRECTIONS

BAG

CO 72 sts. Pm and join for working in the rnd, being careful not to twist. Work in Half Linen Stitch until piece measures approximately 8 1/2" (21.5 cm) from beg, ending with Rnd 2 of pattern.

TOP ROUNDS

Rnd 1 (eyelet round): *K2, yo, k2tog; rep from * around.

Rnd 2: Knit.

Rnd 3: Work Rnd 4 of Half Linen Stitch.

Rnds 4-5: Knit.

Rnd 6: Purl.

BO knitwise.

TIES (MAKE 2)

CO 3 sts. Make 24" (61 cm) long I-cord.

Step: 3

FINISHING

Weave in ends.

With WS facing, place bag flat with beginning of rnd at side fold. Sew center 5" (12.7 cm) of cast-on edges together.

Fold remaining open edges in toward center seam to create lines perpendicular to center seam. Sew these cast-on edges together.

With RS facing and beginning on one side, thread one tie in and out through eyelets around bag. Thread second tie through eyelets beginning from opposite side. Tie ends of each tie together.

Step: 4

LARGE FLOWER

With A and circular needle, CO 86 sts. Do not join.

Row 1: Knit.

Row 2: With B, k1, (k3tog) to last st, k1—30 sts.

Row 3: Purl.

Row 4: Knit.

BO purlwise. Cut yarn, leaving a 12" (30 cm) tail.

Roll cast-on edge of flower into a spiral to form base of flower. Sew edges together.

Step: 5

SMALL FLOWER

With B and circular needle, CO 50 sts. Do not join.

Row 1: Purl.

Row 2: K1, (k3tog) to last st, k1—18 sts.

Row 3: Purl.

BO knitwise. Cut yarn, leaving a 12" (30 cm) tail.

Roll cast-on edge of flower into a spiral to form base of flower. Sew edges together.

Sew flowers to bag in desired location.

Pillow

Materials you'll need:

- 1 skein Red Heart Super Saver in Pumpkin (worsted weight acrylic yarn)
- US size 8 knitted needles
- 16 x 16 inch Pillow form
- Yarn needle
- US size I crochet hook (optional)

Step 1:

Cast on 60 stitches

Knit across all rows until your piece measures 23.5 inches from cast on edge. Bind off and secure loose ends.

My finished piece measured 23.5 inches long by 14 inches wide.

Step 2:

Fold piece in half, with cast on side and bind off side touching. It really shouldn't matter what side is the right or wrong side because garter stitch looks the same on the front and back, but if you have a side that looks better have it on the inside with the ugly side facing outward.

Step 3:

Stitch up the right side, secure yarn, and then stitch up the left side and secure yarn.

You can either stitch up the sides with a yarn needle or use a crochet hook and slip stitch the sides together, I prefer using the crochet hook because it gives a clean seam look.

Step 4:

After sides are connected turn the cover right side out, and it should look like the photo, with the cast on and bind off edge open.

Step 5:

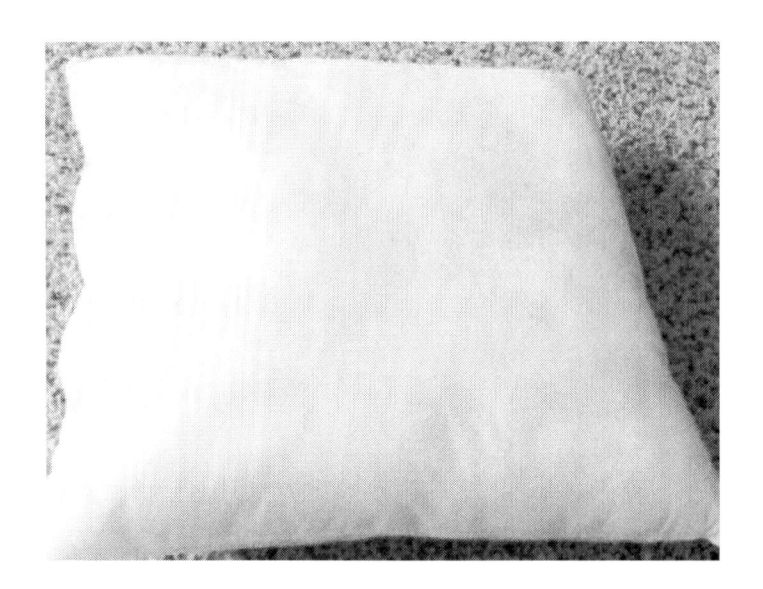

Note: The knit cover will be a lot smaller than the pillow and thats okay because it stretches a lot.

Grab your pillow form and stuff it into knitted cover, smoothing and filling out pillow corners.

Seasonal Knits

Step 6:

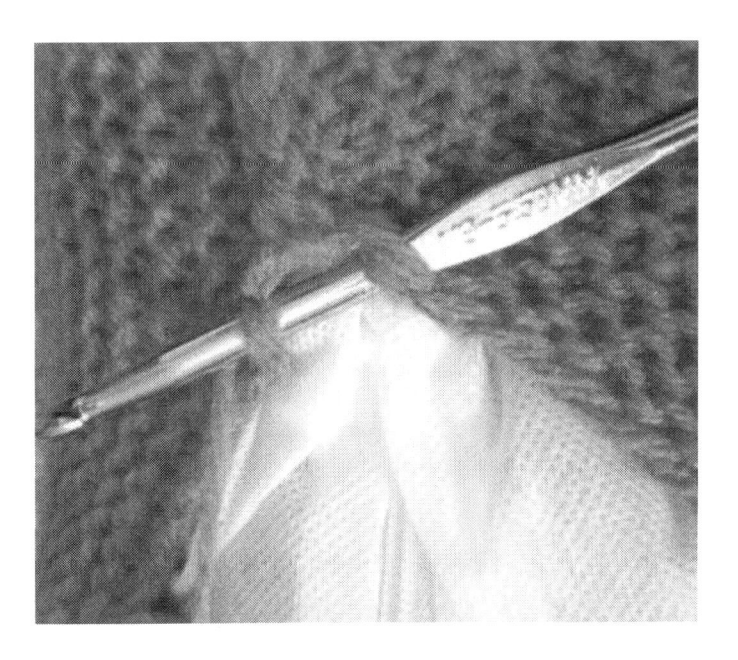

Use the crochet hook again to slip stitch the bottom sides of pillow together. This seam will be a little visible but thats okay because its at the bottom of the pillow and you cant really see it anyways.

Step 7:

This is the finished bottom seam.

Step 8:

Fluff up your pillow, karate chop the top center and place on your favorite chair!

Tank

Step 1: Choose Your Yarn & Needles

I used Bernat Satin Solids in "ebony" for this knit piece (yarn pictured is the same, but in pink).

Although knitting this tank does not demand the use of circular knitting needles, I prefer them, so that's what I used. I used metal circular needs in size US 8 (5.0 mm), despite the yarn recommendation of a US 6.

Step 2: Front of Tank

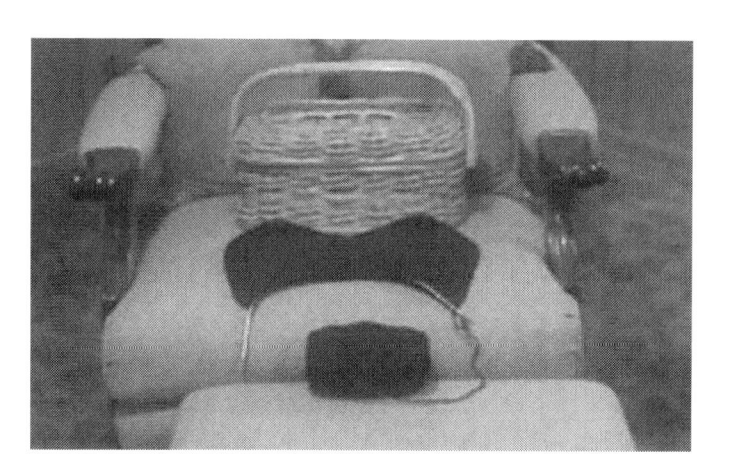

This knit tank was knit in two main pieces (front and back) and then sewn together. It was not knit in the round.

Start with the front piece (top), and cast on 4 stitches. Using a simple garter stitch, knit one stitch, followed by a yarn over, then knit every stitch until the end of the row, and repeat this back and forth until you have 30 stitches on your needle, then snip your yarn leaving enough of a tail to weave in.

Cast on another 4 stitches and repeat the process until you have another 30 stitches on your needle, for a total of 60 stitches.

Knit from one side to the other (continuing normally), but when you get to the end of one knit piece, start picking up the other 30 stitches for a total of 60 continual stitches on the needles.

Knit back and forth (still simple garter stitch), until it's long enough to your liking.

In other words....:

FRONT

-CO 4 (used 16" circular needle, but this isn't a project that needs to be knit in the round)
-K1 YO K to end of row & repeat back and forth until 30 sts on needle, snip yarn leaving enough of a tail to weave in
-Keep yarn on needle & CO another 4
-K1 YO K to end of row until another 30 sts on needle for a total of 60 sts on needle
-Knit from one side picking up the other 30 sts for 60 sts total and knit back and forth until long enough

Step 3: Back of Tank

For the back of the tank, cast on 60 stitches and garter stitch back and forth until it's long enough for your liking.

BACK
-CO 60
-Knit every stitch back and forth until it's long enough to match the front

Step 4: Finishing Details

STRAPS

-I-cords

FINISHING

-Stitch up the sides and straps based on personal fit
-Weave in the ends

Fall

Dishcloth

Step 1: Supplies and Stitches

This is the easiest dishcloth pattern out there and you aren't going to need much to make it.

Supplies:

- Cotton yarn of choice - since this is a dishcloth/washcloth, you want 100% cotton, mercerized cotton should work as well; both single and variegated colors work for this pattern
- Knitting needles size 7 (sizes 5 - 7 should work, the end size of your washcloth will depend on the needles you have, how tight or loose you want the stitches, and how thick or thin your yarn is)

- Counter (optional) - this can be helpful with keep track of stitches or rows. I didn't use it so much for this pattern, but there are future patterns I plan to make where this can be handy to have
- Yarn Needle (not pictured)

Stitches you need to know:

- Cast On (CO)
- Knit (K)
- Yarn Over (yo)
- Knit 2 Together (k2tog)
- Cast off (CO)

Seasonal Knits

Step 2: Pattern

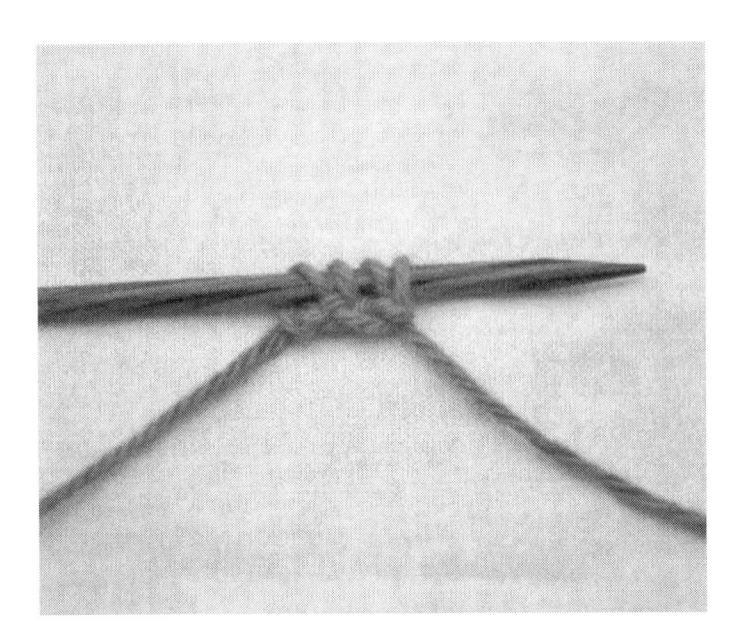

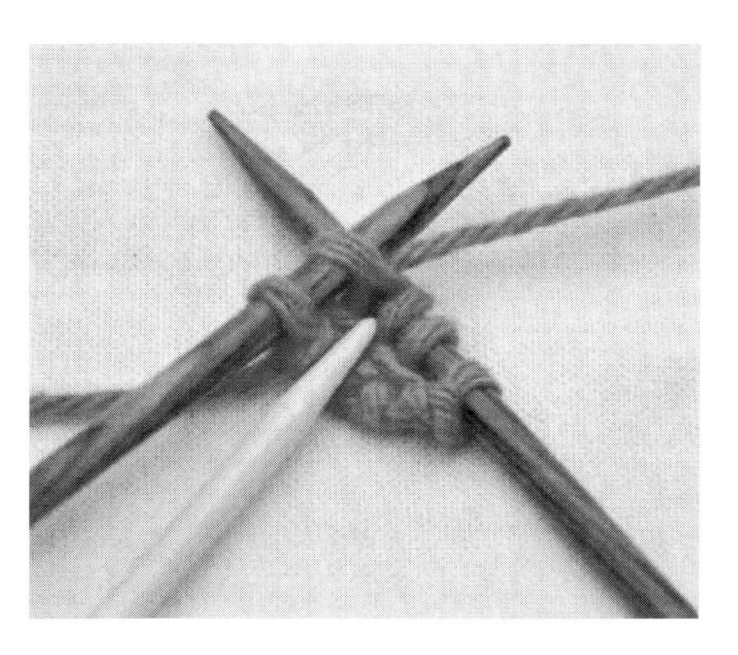

6 More Images

This pattern is pretty easy. You only need to know how to do a couple rows and then you pretty much repeat the rest of the time.

With the counts below, I ended up with a dishcloth that is about 6½"x6½". If you want a bigger one, just continue to increase until the sides are your desired dimensions.

Pattern:

1. CO 4
2. K 4

3.   K 2, yo, knit to end

Repeat step 3 until you have 45 stitches across (or however many you want, it will depend on your needles and yarn size, as you can see in the pictures above, mine ended up having about a 9" diagonal with 6.5" sides).

4.   K 1, k2tog, yo, k2tog, knit to end

Repeat step 4 until you are down to 4 stitches

5.   CO

When you are done, just put the end of the yarn through your last loop, tighten it, and then hide both your ends.

How this pattern works is, each time you yarn over you are creating that "hole" along the edge of the dishcloth while also increasing each row by 1 stitch.

The reason you knit 2 together twice as you decrease is so you can continue to do the yarn over and continue the "hole" border while also decreasing 1 stitch for each row.

Step 3: Make 'em and Use 'em

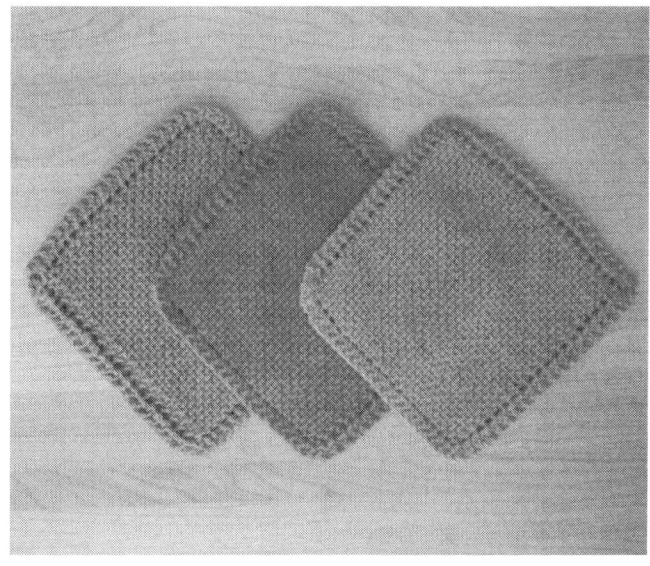

Or give them as gifts. Everyone needs dishcloths and washcloths.

Pumpkin

Supplies:

1/2 skein super thick yarn

size 13 knitting needles

darning needle

poly fiber stuffing

brown scrap fabric (approx 4 in by 10 in)

normal needle

black thread

Hot glue gun

Step 1: Knitting the Pumpkin

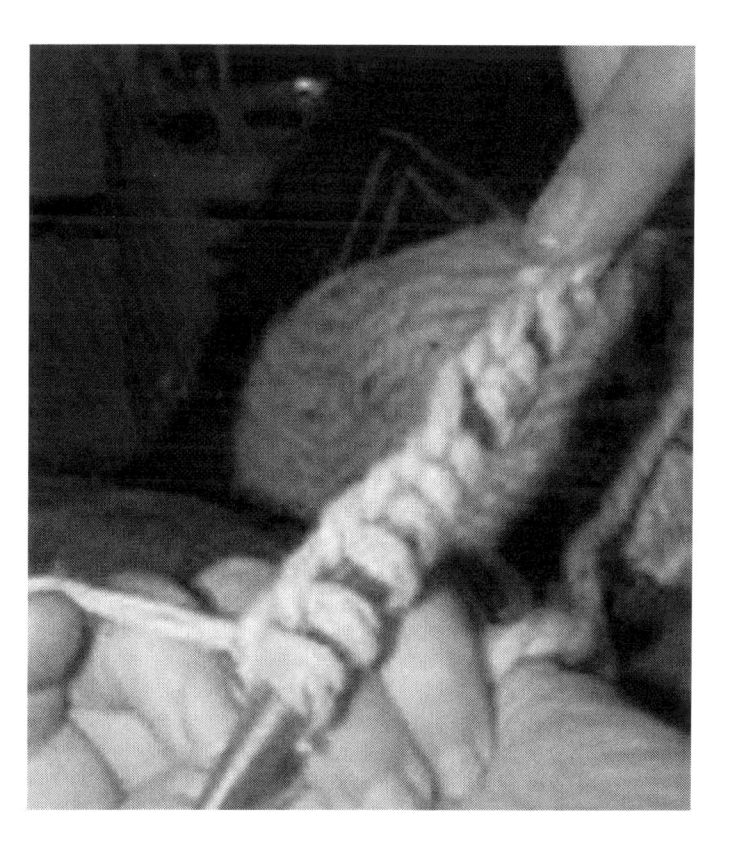

We will knit a rectangle using a ribbed pattern. The ribs resemble the bumps that pumpkins have.

Cast on 30 stitches.

row 1 *Knit two, purl two. repeat from * for the rest of the row

row 2 *Purl two, knit two repeat from * for rest of the row.

Continue to repeat this pattern until you have 20 rows (counting the cast on).

Cast off while continuing the pattern on the 21st row.

Leave a tail approximately 12 in long.

**The size of these pumpkins can be adjusted as desired. When casting on, cast stitches in multiples of 4 plus 2 extra stitches. Knit as many rows until you think it is as long as you want. Remember that is is curved though so just because your piece is x in long doesn't mean your pumpkin will be x in tall when its finished!

Step 2: Sew Up the Pumpkin

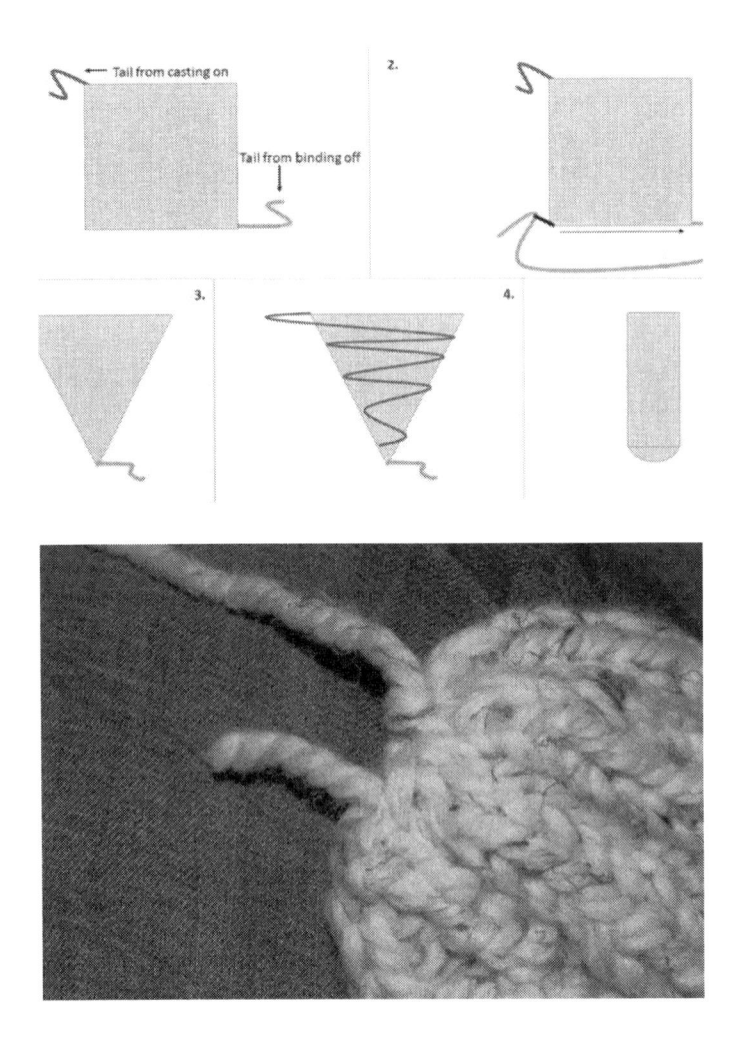

Take the tail of the square and put it through a large darning needle. Thread the tail through the other end of the and weave the tail through the bottom stitch back towards the beginning of the tail. Once you have the tail back to where it started, pull the tail tight to draw the entire end together. Take the remaining tail and stitch in a star pattern until you have securely stitched the end together. This will be the bottom of the pumpkin.

Take the tail from casting on and put through a large darning needle. Line up the two sides so they are even and begin stitching the two sides together by weaving in and out of the two pieces. Stitch the sides all the way to the end.

Tie the remaining end and beginning tails together to ensure they are secured.

Step 3: Fill the Pumpkin and Sew Up

Stuff the pumpkin until its nice and full with a round shape.

Take a new piece of yarn approximately 12 in and put a large darning needle on one end. Loop through one stitch and tie a knot so the yarn does not put through. Begin weaving the yarn through the top stitches around the circle. Once you have reached where you started, pull the yarn tight as before. Stitch in a star pattern until the top of the pumpkin is stitched shut.

Step 4: Adding the Stem

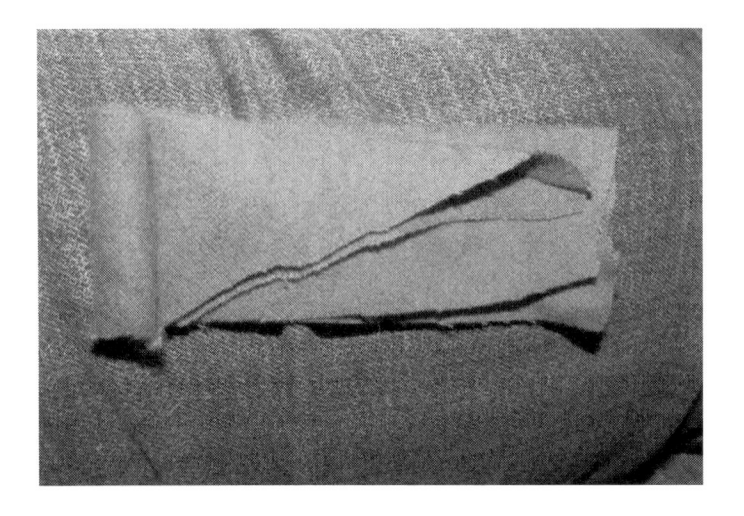

Take a piece of brown fabric and double over hotdog style (i.e. fold the shorter edge in half!) Don't worry if its perfectly square. It is literally just any piece of scrap fabric you have!

Starting at one end of the fabric, begin rolling it up.

Once you have rolled the entire fabric piece up, stitch the end down with a small needle and black thread until it is secured.

Glue stem to the top of the pumpkin. Feel free to add a little leaf or leave it off!

Viola, super easy knitted pumpkin! Enjoy!

Baby Sweater

Materials

- 2 skeins Lion Brand Vanna's Choice in shade 158 Mustard, or 220 yards chunky yarn of your choice
- 1 pair size 9 US (5.5 mm) knitting needles
- 4 duffel coat toggles
- Scissors and yarn needle for finishing

Gauge

3.5 stitches and 8 rows per inch in garter stitch.

Size

Preemie (Newborn, 3 months, 6 months). The instructions show the smallest size with larger sizes in parentheses.

- Chest size finished garment: 14 (16, 18, 20.5) inches
- Length from back neck: 7.5 (8.5, 9.5, 11) inches

Sweater Back

With size 9 needles, cast on 24 (28, 32, 36) stitches.

Work in Garter Stitch (knit every row) until piece measures 4.75 (5.5, 6, 7) inches.

Bind off 3 (3, 4, 4) stitches at the beginning of next 2 rows. There are 18 (22, 24, 28) stitches remaining.

Continue to work in Garter Stitch until piece measures 7.5 (8.5, 9.5, 11) inches.

Bind off.

Fronts

There are two front pieces to this sweater: one with buttons and one with the buttonholes.

First Front

With size 9 needles, cast on 16 (18, 22, 24) stitches.

Work in Garter Stitch until piece measures 4.75 (5.5, 6, 7) inches.

Bind off 3 (3, 4, 4) stitches at the beginning of next row. This is the armhole edge. There are 13 (15, 18, 20) stitches remaining.

Continue to work in Garter Stitch until piece measures 6 (7, 7.5, 8.5) inches, ending at the edge opposite the bound off stitches.

Bind off 9 (10, 12, 12) stitches at beginning of next row. This is the neck edge. There are 4 (5, 6, 8) stitches remaining, which you continue to knit for the shoulder.

Continue to work in Garter Stitch until piece measures 7.5 (8.5, 9.5, 11) inches from cast-on edge to top of shoulder.

Bind off.

Second Front

Work as written for the first front until piece measures 3 (3.25, 3.5, 4.25) inches.

Make buttonholes as follows: Knit 1, knit 2 together, yarn over, knit 4 (5, 5, 6), K2tog, yo, knit to end. The buttonholes are formed closest to the neck edge, opposite to the armhole edge.

Continue to work in Garter Stitch until piece measures 4.75 (5.5, 6, 7) inches, ending at the armhole edge.

Bind off 3 (3, 4, 4) stitches at the beginning of next row. There are 13 (15, 18, 20) stitches remaining.

Next row, make buttonholes: K1, K2tog, yo, K4 (5, 6, 6), K2tog, yo, K to end.

Continue to work in Garter Stitch until piece measures 6 (7, 7.5, 8.5) inches, ending at the edge opposite the bound off stitches.

Bind off 9 (10, 12, 12) stitches at beginning of next row. This is the neck edge. There are 4 (5, 6, 8) stitches remaining, which you continue to knit for the shoulder.

Continue to work in Garter Stitch until piece measures 7.5 (8.5, 9.5, 11) inches from cast-on edge to top of shoulder.

Bind off.

Sleeves

With size 9 needles, cast on 20 (21, 25, 28) stitches.

Work in Garter Stitch until piece measures 5 (6, 7, 8) inches.

Bind off.

Make the second sleeve in the same way.

Assembling

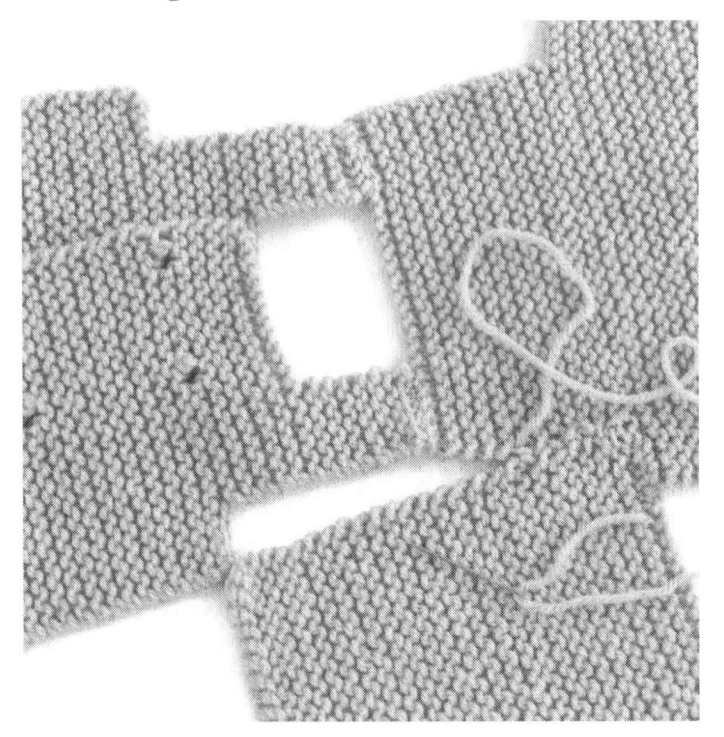

If this is your first sweater-type garment, note that this is the order for finishing on most garments like this. It is normal at this time to block your pieces—either before or after sewing, whatever your preference—but the acrylic yarn does not benefit much from blocking. Washing the sweater in a gentle cycle, however, and then pulling the piece into shape according to the schematic and letting it dry flat will always improve the overall look.

Use yarn for all the sewing.

- Sew the shoulder seams by joining the tops of the fronts to the top of the back. Remember to position the fronts according to where the buttonholes are—left for a girl and right for a boy as you look at it.
- Sew the sleeves into the armholes.
- Sew the side and sleeve seams.

Finishing the Baby Sweater

Weave in all the ends of the yarn.

Sew the toggle buttons in place with yarn, matching the location with the yarn over buttonholes.

For a cute finish, cuff the sleeves.

Winter

Beanie

Supplies

- 1 skein Cascade 220 Heathers
- 16 inch US 8/5 mm circular needles or size needed to get 9 stitches and 12 rows over 2 inches in stockinette
- Stitch marker
- Yarn needle
- Scissors
- Measuring tape

1. Knit the Brim

Cast on 96 stitches, place marker, and join in the round.

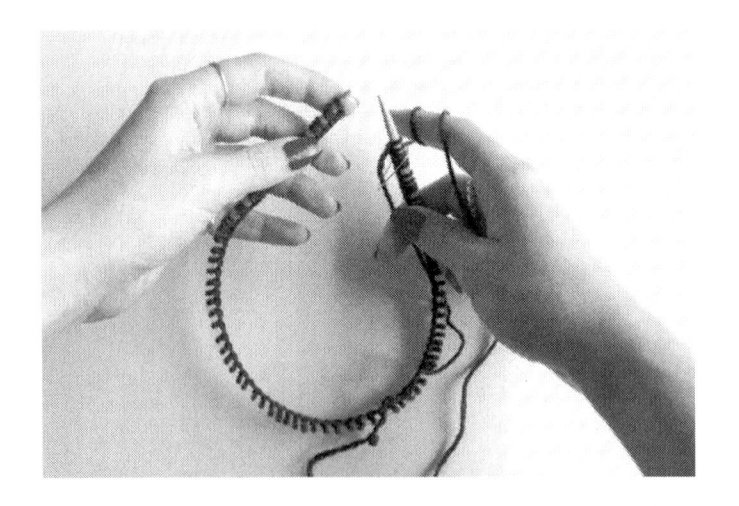

- Round 1: *P2, k2; repeat from * to the end of the round.

- Repeat Round 1 29 more times or until the piece measures approximately 5 inches.

- Round 31: Knit to the end of the round.

- Round 32: *P3, k1; repeat from * to the end of the round.

- Repeat Rounds 31-32 14 more times or until the piece measures approximately 10 inches.

2. Knit the Crown

- Round 61: [K10, k2tog] 8 times. 88 stitches.
- Round 62: [P3, k1] twice, p1, k2tog] 8 times. 80 stitches.
- Round 63: [K8, k2tog] 8 times. 72 stitches.
- Round 64: [P3, k1, p3, k2tog] 8 times. 64 stitches.
- Round 65: [K6, k2tog] 8 times. 56 stitches.
- Round 66: [P3, k1, p1, k2tog] 8 times. 48 stitches.
- Round 67: [K4, k2tog] 8 times. 40 stitches.
- Round 68: [P3, k2tog] 8 times. 32 stitches.
- Round 69: [K2, k2tog] 8 times. 24 stitches.
- Round 70: [P1, k2tog] 8 times. 16 stitches.
- Round 71: K2tog 8 times. 8 stitches.
- Round 72: K2tog 4 times. 4 stitches.

3. Finishing Up

Step 1

With four stitches still on your needle, cut your yarn leaving a long tail. Using the yarn needle, run the yarn through the four stitches and slip them off your needle.

Step 2

Pull the tail tight to gather the crown of the hat. Tie off your yarn to secure.

Step 3

Weave in ends on the wrong side of the hat, and block your project.

Scarf

Materials Needed

- Yarn
- Needles
- Scissors
- A crochet hook (for weaving in the ends)

Buy one skein of super-bulky yarn (size 6 in the Craft Yarn Council's Standard Yarn Weight System), which should be around 100 yards. Lion Brand Wool-Ease Thick and Quick is a nice choice. Use two skeins if you want a longer scarf. The larger the yarn and the lighter the color, the easier it will be to see your stitches.

You will also need size 13 US (9 mm) knitting needles or whatever size creates the gauge you want. It is also helpful to have a crochet hook. With bulky yarn, it is easier to weave in the ends of the yarn with a hook rather than a needle.

Pattern Gauge and Scarf Size

Gauge tells you how many stitches there are per inch. It's affected by the yarn weight, needle size, and your knitting tension. With the suggested yarn and needle combination for this project, you should get around 2 1/2 stitches per inch in garter stitch. If changing yarn weight, you should also change the needle size to get that yarn's recommended gauge.

The finished scarf is about 5 inches wide, but the length will vary depending on the yardage of your chosen yarn and exactly how long you want to make it.

Garter Stitch Scarf Pattern

Knit this entire scarf pattern with a garter stitch. It is nothing more than repeating the basic knit stitch over and over again. That's why it's the perfect beginner's project! By the end of this scarf, you will have this knit stitch down pat and be ready to learn the next stitch.

To create a scarf using the garter stitch, follow these steps:

1. Cast on 12 stitches. This will give you a scarf that's almost 5 inches wide, but you can alter the number of stitches for a wider or narrower scarf. There are a few different ways to cast-on—you can use a long-tail cast-on or try the simple wrap cast on.
2. Knit every stitch and every row with the same garter stitch until you have about a yard of yarn left, or the scarf has reached your desired length. You can also add a new ball of yarn to extend the length or add a different color.
3. Next, you need to bind off.
4. Cut the yarn, leaving a tail of about 6 inches.
5. Use your crochet hook to weave in the ends at the top and the bottom, as well as any extra ends if you added a second ball of yarn.

Leg Warmers

Things You'll Need

- Worsted-weight yarn, any color
- Set of U.S. size 8 straight knitting needles
- Set of U.S. size 9 straight knitting needles
- Embroidery needle

Step 1

Cast 30 stitches onto the size-8 knitting needles.

Step 2

Knit one stitch, purl one stitch until you have worked your piece for 3 inches from the knitting needle.

Step 3

Switch to size-9 knitting needles and knit in stockinette stitch -- knit one whole row, purl one whole row repeatedly -- until your leg warmer is the desired length, minus 3 inches. The side that shows the knit stitch will be the outside of the leg warmer, or right side.

Step 4

The last 3 inches, switch back to the size 8 knitting needles, return to the knit 1 stitch, purl 1 stitch and repeat the pattern.

Step 5

Bind off loosely after completing 3 inches of this pattern.

Step 6

Fold the leg warmer lengthwise with the knitted side on the inside. Sew together using the same color yarn and embroidery needle. Turn the leg warmer right side out.

Step 7

Repeat Steps 1 through 6 for the second leg warmer.

Printed in Great Britain
by Amazon